THE FINEST TUNING

302 Haiku

Franklin Magalhães

001 - Pencil and paper –
always peering at the verse
as a paparazzo.

002 - Church of black men –
believers of all colors
in worship.

003 - Rio summer –
at noon, a block is almost
a journey.

004 - It's after midnight
children playing in the street.
Tropical summer.

005 - A tall tree reigns
well above the mangoes.
Kingbird's watchtower.

006 - Dressed cages –
fools take their birds
for a walk.

007 - Blue skies.
Not even a cloud
to hide a UFO.

008 - Chainsaw noise.
Bird's nest and chirps
are gone...

009 - Turns on... turns off...
Flying in the darkness,
a firefly.

010 - Old church,
nine saints on duty.
Good attendance!

011 - Rainy dusk.
Coming out the clouds
plane's lights.

012 - A flying at dusk.
Did pass a bat
or a late pigeon?

013 - Full moon.
The old wolf awakens
within the little poodle.

014 - Waving kites.
Against the reddening sky,
shape of palm trees.

015 - The last lightning.
There are no more thunders
nor raindrops.

016 - My pulse
and the wall clock.
Total synchronism.

017 - Rain over.
In the dripping wires,
Babel of sparrows.

018 - Summer night.
While watering the garden,
feeding mosquitoes.

019 - Point to the stress.
The kitten has pooped
in the Zen garden.

020 - At the red light,
awaiting permission to
continue living.

021 - Observing the sky.
The trail of the plane is
a cloud now.

022 - Shadow and freshwater.
The ferns are having good times
bordering the well.

023 - A tiny star
entangled in my hair.
Flower of mango.

024 - Party on the lawn.
Ants parading flags
and wealthy trophies.

025 - Lady's cell phone
matching her eyes.
Sunday at the mall.

026 - My father's look,
forty years later,
within the mirror.

027 - Flying seeds.
Who has said the trees
can't fly?

028 - Winter night.
In the memory, the bonfires
never snuff out.

029 - It is a real luxury.
Snails outline their paths
with silver ink.

030 - Sing, robin!
At these so glad mornings,
why be silent?

031 - Fall morning.
Amidst the thick mist,
the world disappeared.

032 - Surprise in the road.
The fog brought the night
into the afternoon.

033 - Weightless gem
floats in the wind.
Soap bubble.

034 - Sky on fire and
the asphalt burning feet.
One more popsicle!

035 - Modern slaves.
Faith, promises and wishes
in the black men church.

036 - There's a swallow
sleeping on the altar.
Tiny nun.

037 - Trail in the forest.
Birdies and agoutis
collecting seeds.

038 - The clay chimney
seems to slide.
Passing clouds.

039 - By midafternoon,
our star took a nap.
Solar eclipse.

040 - Freshly mown grass.
Four cats in a row
check the job.

041 - A scream in the forest.
In a dried high branch,
a bird watches.

042 - Backyard party.
Stars blinking over
the cold town.

043 - Cold June night.
The far echoes from
country dancing.

044 - Father's Day.
Socks, ties and laughs,
all the Sunday.

045 - Windy autumn and leaves
in the desert streets.
Endless running.

046 - Hidden treasure.
Under the big green leaves,
yam roots.

047 - So dark night...
The clouds, shyly,
dressed the moon.

048 - A dog chases me
through the deserted night.
It's sniffing a friend.

049 - Who will be blamed
if, despite the tiredness,
the dream didn't come?

050 - Sad goodbye.
Tears were much more than
a speck in the eye.

051 - Insomnia brings me
to the night round.
The dogs salute me.

052 - Thick eastern clouds
already getting red.
Insomnia won.

053 - A friend goes by
fighting against the sleep.
"-Good morning, guy!"

054 - In a lack of flowers,
a bouquet of caladiums.
Autumn Sunday.

055 - Lilac bougainvillea.
Even forgotten in a corner
still blossoms.

056 - So many dry leaves!...
Walking over a carpet
of old memories.

057 - Sudden wind.
An unfinished poem flies
through the window.

058 - Back to childhood.
Smell of steam engines,
gooseberry taste...

059 - Disappointing harvest.
Any blackberry for
the pie filling.

060 - Your warm hug
at the first Sun of June.
My birthday.

061 - Barks all night.
The moon seems to play
hide and seek.

062 - Hellish heat.
Drinking on the same glass
one bee and me.

063 - The roaring of a train
over the iron bridge.
The day is coming.

064 - Far away from home,
Okinawa cherry blossoming
one more time.

065 - Near thunderbolt.
The kitten has splashed
its milk bowl.

066 - Smart eyes
learn how Grandpa
peels oranges.

067 - Enchanted night.
Ferns watch the fairies
dancing.

068 - Fierce night.
The sails are defying the sea.
So far is the pier...

069 - Intriguing reading.
Night came on and slowly broke
into the room.

070 - Strained atoms
seeking a purpose.
Big Bang's legacy.

071 - It's raining in the bonsai.
Snails are interbreeding
in no hurry.

072 - Nests on alert.
Hawks are flying close to
the treetops.

073 - All the time,
furniture makes noises.
Sleepless night.

074 - Grandma visit.
Peanut candy, souvenir
from the farm.

075 - Cold drizzling
in midsummer of Rio.
The swallows fly.

076 - In the convent sky,
a flock of swallows.
Flying nuns?

077 - In the palm tree,
a robin welcomed the day.
Good neighbor.

078 - Cloud of termites.
At the spring nights,
not all are flowers.

079 - The cold breeze brings
sweet smells of the night.
Gardenia... jasmine...

080 - The tiredness of the day.
Amidst chirps and colors,
the afternoon ends.

081 - Colors festival.
Butterflies giving a show
from garden to garden.

082 - Brisk visit.
Hummingbirds reflecting
the Sun.

083 - Painfully
the blades of grass rise.
The match is over.

084 - A rainy carnival.
Wet pooches and sad harlequins
at the tavern door.

085 - No letters today.
The postman crosses the road
for a handshake.

086 - Slow sunset.
A bonsai goes growing
in its shadow.

087 - Scalding sand.
The tiny crabs do not venture
out of their lairs.

088 - Sparrows say goodbye.
So nostalgic are the bells
of Ave Maria!...

089 - A slight trembling.
The gray floor gets covered
with white petals.

090 - The weather changed.
Clothes running away,
following the wind.

091 - Breeze ruffling
the surface of the lake.
Another leaf falls.

092 - Another day ends.
The cicadas are lighting
their sunny songs.

093 - The time has frozen
in the wings of a hummingbird.
The rain... the wind...

094 - Rainstorm in the hills.
Under the blooming tree,
the goats scream.

095 - Rain and lighting.
There are curtains of diamonds
on the edge of the roof.

096 - Dragonflies hover
and bathing in the pool.
The girl floats.

097 - A new bike.
In his birthday, the boy
is all smiles.

098 - Another hummingbird.
Or an old customer
coming back?

099 - Old pages...
Dried petals of a rose,
My young days.

100 - Ink running out.
My pen enough for
one more haiku.

101 - Between the writing hand
and the furtive thinking
all the words.

102 - Under the blankets,
third age games for two –
"How many letters?"

103 - This masquerade –
a gift for the faces
little blessed.

104 - Barefoot in the grass –
remembering the rain
of childhood.

105 - Wind resistance –
tendrils of creepers
held hands.

106 - Blank Sunday –
nobody to a smart chat,
even me.

107 - Thirty-eight degrees –
a slap killed the sweat
walking on my leg.

108 - Insomnia haiku –
forgotten masterpiece
when the sun rises.

109 - Remanent flowers –
my little girl tells them
spring is over.

110 - Deep sleeping.
Would prefer to have been
kindly awakened.

111 - Gallstones –
deep down, she accuses me
for them too.

112 - A cut in time
with full autonomy –
haiku flavor.

113 - Do flowers not speak?!
Learn the language of colors,
the gift of perfumes!

114 - Faith Market –
crutches *prêt à porter*
to overcome fear.

115 - My mind and yours,
the Center of the Cosmos –
and yours, and yours.

116 - Favorable winds –
the high flight is possible
with kigo offline.

117 - Charmless life –
How lucky the girls
I didn't marry!

118 - So mild morning
and the coffee came out perfect!
Too bad to be alone.

119 - Spring visits,
but never welcome.
Termite clouds.

120 - Vacant time.
On the blackboard
a chalk haiku.

121 - Your face
before turning off the light –
Sweet dreams in sight!

122 - Nothing impossible –
in a strange dream,
I run away from my idol.

123 - Not so bad at all –
hummingbirds and butterflies
will inherit the Earth.

124 - Sudden stop –
a brake to rearrange
this crazy world.

125 - A scythe –
I know nothing about the moon,
only when it is full.

126 - Nine rebirths –
my children and theirs
perpetuating me.

127 – Just now,
I allowed myself to cry –
It didn't help much...

128 - Lives that go.
The timeless presence
of river stones.

129 – This quarantine –
I shaved my old mask,
but let it grow soon!

130 - Quarantine –
that second honeymoon
long dreamed.

131 - Facebook pals,
more precious than ever!
Pandemia times.

132 - Keeping clearness –
my haiku only leave home
after showering.

133 – It looked
pure old-fashioned greed,
but it was evil.

134 - Haïku face –
My wife realizes
when I'm composing.

135 - Bits and bytes only –
to the micro, doesn't matter
it is a love letter.

136 - Starry night –
my insignificance
at full size.

137 - Harvesting bananas –
my son has no idea that
reminds me of Basho.

138 - Sundown –
ice cubes go melting
in the drink.

139 - Cobweb –
everything caught
but food.

140 - Christmas camping –
My Holy Family
remembering The Crib.

141 - December 30 –
almost not born on time
for New Year.

142 - Pool photos -
remembering the summer
to exorcise the cold.

143 - Late Autumn –
no more sparkles in her eyes
when she sees me.

144 - Men and animals –
implacable Africa
forging lives.

145 – Flowers in the pool –
the unexpected beauty
after the storm.

146 - Too much rain –
there are plants considering
become fishes.

147 - Fully wrapped –
Is she just going to sleep
or become a butterfly?

148 - Spree on the bed!
The wife slept over
at her sister's home.

149 - Suffocation –
What tight tie!
So far is Sunday.

150 - My poem
on the tip of the pen.
Eager by moonrise.

151 - Overcast day.
Only the clock is knowing
about noon.

152 - Circumnavigation.
My Magellanic haiku
follows the daybreak.

153 - Around the world.
A flock of haiku flying
toward the sunrise.

154 - Late afternoon –
it is the first cicada
I hear this year.

155 - Upon the edge –
even about the weather,
the choked voice up.

156 - Amazing irony –
after I reclused at home,
I've got more friends.

157 - Young's love –
hummingbirds get lost
among the flowers.

158 - Family Sunday –
Monday, washing the dishes
in a good mood.

159 – In the spider's house,
turn on, turn off, turn on.
Request for help.

160 - Tropical Paradise –
The joy of a sunbath
at any season.

161 - Modern slaves –
Faith, promises, and frustrations,
in fake churches.

162 - Great kiskadee –
it also suffers
from the heat.

163 - Double citizenship.
My wife hates the time
I spent on the Moon!

164 - Locked at home –
free on the streets, viruses
and stray bullets.

165 - Alone on a rainy day –
do resist, let the sleep
to the empty night.

166 - Woke by the rain –
his eyes did not agree,
he slept again.

167 - Direct effect
of the rain of stars –
a haijin was born!

168 - The rain and the cold
inspired the sparrow –
It looks like Vivaldi!

169 - Sublimated –
her taste still pervades
the memory.

170 - Crossing the 70s –
Since childhood,
well with Life.

171 - Madness reigns –
to maintain my sanity,
I write haiku.

172 - Strangers in the street -
maybe best friends
from kindergarten.

173 - Post-cath mood:
in my soul,
Fred meets Ginger!

174 - Chest cleaning –
fits a lot more people now
in this heart.

175 - Looking at the moon –
suddenly
a shooting star!

176 - Feet on the ground,
looking up to heaven –
yearning for freedom.

177 - Yearning for freedom
a dreaming horse
becomes a Pegasus.

178 - A dreamer,
yearning for freedom
rises to the skies.

179 - Nature contrasts –
softness and beauty
of vultures flight.

180 - The journey of tears -
as long as
the dimples cheek.

181 - Shooting star –
at last a warm cradle
to resting.

182 - Long ago… Maktub!
The blessings of Basho
before we met.

183 - Predawn,
the world returns –
another jet.

184 - Hard insomnia!
Depression creeps in,
but soon it goes.

185 - Night of insomnia –
Depression makes fun,
I free me from it!

186 - Inflated Ego –
since no one praises me,
I try to deceive myself.

187 - Kill to eat –
fire use, it disguises
the beast we are.

188 - Here comes the Sun!
Street lamps turned off
in reverence.

189 - Birthday eve,
and I cannot sleep –
prenatal tension.

190 - Lovely rivals –
the flirt of Nature
with my love.

191 - Almost lost day -
nothing more useful than
watering the plants.

192 - Facebook pals –
stamps collection
no more.

193 - Near expiry date -
I have saved several beers
from a useless life.

194 - Somewhere
my Quantum twin writes
this same haiku.

195 - Lost in the night -
the big eyes of a moth
on my pillow.

196 - Ecological poet –
he only uses
second-hand words.

197 - Soaked night –
I thought the clay frog
would jump out.

198 - Autumn storm –
the bulging eyes
of the clay frog.

199 - The gift of languages –
plants and animals reveal
sacred secrets.

200 - Sudden internment -
in the cardiogram only
love and poetry

201 - A crushed pigeon
on the church clock.
It was time to die.

202 - Times of quarantine –
today is today, I think.
Tomorrow? Too.

203 - In a lack of flowers,
a bouquet of caladiums.
Autumn Sunday.

204 - Full tummy –
the hummingbird
cleans its wings.

205 - Sunny savanna –
the defiant looking
of mom-lioness.

206 - Sleeping protected –
sure weapons within
reach of the mind.

207 - Afternoon nap –
The fan soundtrack,
screams and planes.

208 – "and God created woman."
An affair with Bardot,
in the night of Buzios.

209 - Farm brandy –
the little bee insists on
kissing my lips

210 - Another party end –
someone forgot, of course,
a charger.

211 - Finished job!
The office chair,
a merry-go-round!

212 - Tropical chat –
another sweatdrop
on the cellphone.

213 - Full year and life –
there is one thing missing,
but it's just money.

214 - The Phoenix palm tree,
too much thorny. Not a tree
for a hug.

215- Last Sunset of Spring –
Newborn birds are excited
with their gift of singing.

216 - Premature Summer –
The execrated president
is already ruling ...

217 - Love will win. –
a madman is trying to detain
the Sun rising.

218 - Millenium turnaround –
on the Roof of the World
I've got a friend.

219 – Spring!
Will the brooms miss you,
fallen leaves?

220 - My corner of the world,
better than any other –
kids and grandkids

221 - Sparrow's jam session!
Some mark the beat
others improvise.

222 - Resting in the stone,
the frog blew me off.
Each one in his own.

223 - Sleepless night –
a hormone-filled cricket
swears of love.

224 - Past midnight –
another noisy plane
in my insomnia.

225 - A talk about galaxies,
snails and fireflies,
for the haiku's sake.

226 - Reviewing texts,
listening to *Torna a Sorriento* –
Winter afternoon.

227 - Ancestral Cradle –
Afro-descendants,
wanting it or not.

228 - Old chrome –
the fungi recycling
memories...

229 - Confinement –
following the trail
of sugar ants.

230 - In the garden –
remembering me to Basho,
a cornerstone.

231 - Moonlight walk –
the sweet scent of flowers
and a stolen kiss

232 - Life beyond life –
the drowned fly in the pool
it goes on the flying...

233 - Ikarus' triumph –
in up to 10 installments
on credit card.

234 - The Supermoon –
for the third time
in my life.

235 - Poor man's cam –
I failed to capture
the Supermoon.

236 - Half past midnight –
so brief the meeting
with my Asian friends...

237 - Hollywood musical –
I would like living
so surrealistically!

238 - Improving the evening –
turning off the TV
to enjoy the rain.

239 - Rain and lightning –
There are curtains of diamonds
on the edge of the roof.

240 - Minoan heritage –
forty centuries later,
our sweet Julia.

241 - Aging flow –
just a wink, and it's again
pills time.

242 - Ancient faith –
the stone Master
welcomes the Sun!

243 - Watering the garden –
the scared little chameleon
scared me too.

244 - A party on the lawn –
ants parade flags
and rich trophies.

245 - Winter morning –
just slumped flowers
in the swimming pool

246 - Bats and swallows –
classmates at the same
flight school.

247 - One more dragon
staring at me from the clouds.
Pareidolia

248 - Life secrets –
the girls don't know yet
the grandma, no more

249 - After cutting, revise –
"Me, Tarzan... you, Jane!"
Greystoke haiku.

250 - The light is gone –
forms are going
with the time...

251 - In a Distant Land –
if Shrek goes still far...
Hulk kisses Fiona!

252 - "Come on, boy!"
When cops-and-badmen
It was a child's play.

253 - Feeling sad –
Democracy under attack,
But we go on

254 - Honey for hummingbirds –
all day long waiting
for a good photo.

255 - Photo-hunter –
waiting all-day
for a hummingbird.

256 - Old Patriarch –
accordingly to Hoyle,
bald and bearded.

257 - Following me? Cool!
Maybe my WARP skill
will let you in the vacuum...

258 - Time flies –
again in the shower
washing my briefs.

259 - Lockdown drink –
the tramp wine, never
tasted it so well.

260 - In the web,
dry leaves hanged
spinning.

261 - Dirty pool –
the unexpected beauty
after the storm.

262 - Snake's throat –
the frog slips into
silently

263 - She smiled me –
with help from The Beatles,
a charmed guy.

264 - Evening visits –
the star and the granddaughter –
dolce far niente.

265 - Grass blades –
linked forever
to the poetry.

266 - Man-made comet –
a transcontinental flight
at the dusk.

267 - It's raining in the bonsai –
snails are interbreeding
in no hurry.

268 - Moving home –
the last sunrise
in the old nest.

269 - On the screen,
Debbie's smiling –
my puppy love

270 - Modules of twenty –
I'm a preteen
of module four.

271 - A dead katydid –
Brazilians call it
"hope"

272 - Bare feet –
on the beach sand,
shoelessgraphy.

273 - Cloudy and cold,
the weathergirl said.
I got it: Brandy!

274 - "I started a joke" –
teen years returning
in my wrinkled face.

275 - My bloomy fence –
the frowning neighbor
smiled again.

276 - Neck strain –
all night chasing for
a shooting star.

277 - An angel touched me,
the delicacy of wings –
and not even realized...

278 - A lioness with cub,
tracing the path herself –
the sun in her hair...

279 - Damn coup-plotters
sow hate in the ground
of the poetry!

280 - Flowerless trees –
The birds provide
the lacking colors.

281 - Brexit –
a selfie aiming at
the belly button.

282 - Brexit –
neologism about
egocentrism.

283 - Kindergarten pool –
a frog jumps.
Screams and crying.

284 - So beautiful
my unpleasant town
before dawning.

285 - My garden, its home –
the lizard doesn't even know
it is already my pet.

286 - A-ha moment –
my new "childhood friends"
inside their haiku.

287 - Rio, 40 degrees –
my poor apple tree
never blossomed.

288 - Easter Sunday.
Opening the wings to the Life –
angel or hummingbird?

289 - Mideast refugees –
Europe is tasting
unexpected spices.

290 - Take it on the chin.
Better than hitting head on
with her nerves.

291 - Tropical Christmas –
sweat dripping from
Santa's forehead.

292 - To stand up early –
before the songbird
wake the sun.

293 - Gloomy Sunday –
Two vultures on duty
over the water tower.

294 - A masquerade –
These eyes greeting me,
do I know them?

295 - Bland party –
granddaughter's birthday
and not even a hug.

296 - And life goes on
like a treacherous river,
slowly and inexorably...

297 - Illusory power –
The smallest creatures,
the most deadly.

298 - Almost lost day –
nothing more useful
than watering the plants.

299 - Very happily
they kidnapped the rainbow –
Does Dorothy know?

300 - Realize the irony –
after I reclused at home,
I've got more friends.

301 - Harvesting haiku –
a minimal portion of Life
in my daily way.

302 - Faithful companions –
my old dictionaries
rest on the shelf.